# The Savvy Saver

21 Days to Master Your Money and Save With Confidence

With

## About Me

Hi, my name is Caroline and I live in the United Kingdom with my Husband and our 2 children.

I created The Savvy Saver as saving money has always been a part of who I am and I have learned a lot throughout the years. It's not just about being able to put those pennies away but having the right mindset to do so.

So dive right in and get started!

# Introduction

Welcome and well done for taking the first step to becoming a Savvy Saver.

Over the next 21 days you will work towards understanding your mindset around money and kickstart you on the journey to saving for the things you desire without you going without.

Maybe you understand a little or a lot around money mindset and maybe you just need a refresher, that's fine, you will find something in the next 21 days that will help you

Do you often feel stuck when it comes to saving money

Do you often feel like when you think of money it feels you with dread?

Do you want to improve the way you think about money and start saving with confidence and gratitude?

Maybe you haven't a clue where to start when it comes to being able to save money!

The welcome to The Savvy Saver.

Over 21 days, you will work on three important areas when it comes to your finances.

Firstly, your Mindset. This is where you will dig deep into what you really think,

Then, you move on to dissecting your money. A thing a lot of people feel uncomfortable with.

Lastly, you will put things in to action and take the action needed.

Each task for the day shouldn't take more than 20 minutes

Before we look at ways to save, we need to look around our thoughts around money and dig deep with them.

Money is pretty much a taboo subject. No one really likes talking about it and we just 'get by' but what we think about it makes a difference on how we use it.

The way we think about money is deep ingrained within us. From things we have heard to things we have witnessed growing up. Others relationships and attitudes surrounding money and much more which we will dig deeper to find what your mindset is like around money.

So you will need a pen to mark these pages and possibly a notebook for extra pages (I have added some additional pages here as well) and get ready to answer some deep thought provoking questions!

Don't want you to feel overwhelmed so taking it easy.

You may find other thoughts and feelings come up and that's fine. Note them down too even if they don't seem relevant.

# DAY 1

**Firstly, on a scale of 1-10 (1 being crap, 10 being amazing) how do you feel about money? Write your answer and we will revisit this during the course.**

So the first question we are going to explore is:

## What do you think about money?

What exactly are your thoughts around money? It may be that you feel quite positive and think that having money in your life is a positive aspect. You may think that having enough money and more gives you status within the community.

Or do you think that money is the root of all evil and that people who have more money then you are show off's, up themselves and think they are better then everyone else.

Remember there is no right or wrong answer.

Write your answers down, just whatever comes to your head. There is no need to go deep just yet as we have a lot more to explore over the coming days.

## DAY 2

Growing up we would have all heard our parents talking about money. I remember myself, my mother used to be the book keeper if you like of the household money. She had this book where she would record EVERYTHING that was going in and out. Being one of 7, money was tight when I was growing up. Both my parents worked full time to provide for us, however, conversations around money happened.

When you were growing up, you may have heard your parents or other grown ups discussing money, even when they thought you weren't around.

The classics are "money doesn't grow on trees", "Do you think we are made of money", having hand me downs from your older siblings or having your Mum (in my case my brother but this wasn't to save money) cut your hair.

So today's questions to answer are:

As a child, what were your parents like about money?

Do you find yourself thinking/saying the same way/things?

# DAY 3

Thinking about yesterdays task, I, myself have found myself thinking similar thoughts as my parents. I even hear my husband saying to our Children, "You have to eat that because that's what costs money".

I often say to my Daughter, "do you think we are made of money", "You can't have everything you see, everything costs", and I know where these thoughts have stemmed from. Ingrained in generations and generations. We want our children to grow up and not fear money or live in a lack mindset.

Todays task

Looking at yesterdays answers, do you see a pattern with how you think about money to how your parents thought/discuss? Or have you found yourself thinking differently?

What have you found yourself saying and thinking around money that has come from someone older when you were growing up.

Again, write whatever comes to your head.

# DAY 4

We all have a relationship with money whether we like it or not, so, looking at yours, think about the answers to the past 3 days tasks and answer this question:

Is your relationship with money positive or negative? How would you describe your relationship with money? I love money but it hates me? It comes to me whenever I want and need it to?

Really think about why it is either/or. Write down some examples of when these positive or negative thoughts have come up and how it has affected you.

Remember there is no right or wrong.

## DAY 5

Time to get a little creative and doodle!!

You answered yesterdays question whether your relationship with money is positive or negative. Time to dig a little deeper now.

Question to answer:

If positive - have you ever felt negatively about money and visa versa? If so, when? Task

Draw a spider graph and let everything come out. Was it when you wanted to buy a certain item but didn't have enough money? When you lent a friend some money and never received it back? When you won 3-4 lines on the lotto? Every situation where you have felt positive or negative. Do it in different colours if it helps you.

# DAY 6

Looking at Day 5 and whether you felt positive or negative about money, look at each statement/thing you have written.

On a scale of 1-10 mark next to it how relevant it is to your life right now.

Think about how reading that back and looking at it in black/blue and white really makes you feel.

# DAY 7

There is no denying it, money is an important aspect to life. With everything going up and everything costing no matter what it is, it does hold an important part of our lives, but how important to you let it be to you.

Task:

How important is money to you in your life?

When answering this question, dig deep.

Why is it important to you in this way?

What would be different if it wasn't so important to you?

Do these beliefs around how important it is stem from what you have already discovered so far?

# DAY 8

Looking at the past week, on a scale of 1-10 (1 being crap, 10 being amazing) how do you feel about money now? Do you think your mindset has changed around money?

Do you feel that there is more work to be done? Be honest with yourself and mark your answer down

# DAY 9

We have been spending the past days really looking at your mindset around money. Now we are going to to continue and learn to be grateful for money.

Firstly I would like to introduce an affirmation to you, to use throughout the day. Every morning say this affirmation and if you find yourself stressing or worrying about money, say it:

**I have an abundance of money and am grateful for all money that I receive and pay out. Money comes easy to me and I love and cherish it.**

# TASK

Before we dissect your money. I would like you to figure out how much you would like to save. It can be as big or small as you like.

Why are we doing this first? Because if we work out how much money you have and what you spend, you will look at what you have left and then decide from that what you an realistically save. That's not the best way to do it because you are already coming from a place of lack. We want to come from a place of abundance.

So in a year from now how much would you have liked to save? £500, £1,000, £5,000

Whatever the amount, divide it by 12. This is what you need to save monthly. Break it even more further and divide that by 4 (weekly) and as some months have 30 or 31 days, divide that amount by 31.

Now you will have your yearly goal, what you need to save monthly, weekly and daily. Now say THANK YOU, THANK YOU. THANK YOU for receiving this money. These are your milestones and your steps to keep an eye on your progress and whether you are on target or not.

## DAY 10

Say your affirmation: **I have an abundance of money and am grateful for all money that I receive and pay out. Money comes easy to me and I love and cherish it.**

Following on from yesterday, time to get creative!

Grab a piece of paper and a pen/pencil/crayon if you wish and one the left side of the page, about a CM in, draw a line down. Then draw a line along the bottom about a CM up from the bottom. You can see we are going to graph this.

Next head your paper with the amount you would like to save a year.

As a sub heading you can also put the monthly, weekly and daily amounts as a reminder.

You can do the next step in 2 ways, whichever works best for you.

Next along the bottom write what your yearly amount is but broken down. So for example you want to save £5,000, break it down in to £1,000 or even £500's. Write these along the bottom until they add up to £5k.

Next along the left side, again you can break this down to £50, £100, £200. So every time you have saved this amount, you colour it in and keep adding. You will then get the top which will end in whatever amount is at the bottom and have a graph.

You can also break the bottom line down to whatever it is monthly you need to save and the left side to whatever it is weekly.

Put it up somewhere you will see it everyday.

Say your 3 THANK YOUS for receiving this money.

# DAY 11

Now time to get raw but remember to say your affirmation:

**I have an abundance of money and am grateful for all money that I receive and pay out. Money comes easy to me and I love and cherish it.**

Write all your debts in your notebook. Bank account, credit cards, debts to others, court debts. Everything. You don't need to write the amount, only to whom and for what.

Now your debts are written down, make a list of all your monthly payments. No numbers, just listing.

Say your 3 THANK YOUS but this time this is for these debts. Yes you are saying thank you for being able to have the money, no matter where it came from, to live, to eat and have all the necessities.

## DAY 12

**I have an abundance of money and am grateful for all money that I receive and pay out. Money comes easy to me and I love and cherish it.**

Now, you have a list of all your outgoings, time to write the amounts. Not the amount that you are paying back each month but the total amount of any debt outstanding. Say thank you after each one.

If you don't know them off by heart or exactly then give a good estimate. Dig out your bank statements, old letters to find the exact amounts.

How much do they add up to?

Say your 3 THANK YOUS

# DAY 13

**I have an abundance of money and am grateful for all money that I receive and pay out. Money comes easy to me and I love and cherish it.**

Incoming money. Now you have a list of all your outgoings and how much they add up to, write a list of any regular incomings you have. Wages, commissions (although these can vary so an average), any benefits you receive, regular subscriptions people pay for to you.

Say your 3 THANK YOUS

## DAY 14

**I have an abundance of money and am grateful for all money that I receive and pay out. Money comes easy to me and I love and cherish it.**

Now you have your list of incomings, write down the amount of each, saying thank you after each one.

How much incomings do you receive each month?

Say your 3 THANK YOUS for receiving this money.

# DAY 15

**I have an abundance of money and am grateful for all money that I receive and pay out. Money comes easy to me and I love and cherish it.**

Looking at the past week, on a scale of 1-10 (1 being crap, 10 being amazing) how do you feel about money now? Do you think your mindset has changed around money?

Do you feel that there is more work to be done? Be honest with yourself and mark your answer down

Has it changed since day 8?

# DAY 16

**I have an abundance of money and am grateful for all money that I receive and pay out. Money comes easy to me and I love and cherish it.**

Looking at your outgoings list from day 12, what are the monthly figures you are paying back each month? If you aren't paying anything back then obviously write 0. Again say thank you after each one.

Now add in the amount of savings per month you would like to save (from Day 9) as an outgoing.

How much in total are all your monthly outgoings?

Say your 3 THANK YOUS for this money

# DAY 17

**I have an abundance of money and am grateful for all money that I receive and pay out. Money comes easy to me and I love and cherish it.**

Now you have to be honest and see it all in black and white which can be uncomfortable however, it is necessary to be aware.

Take your outgoings AWAY from your incomings. What are you left with? a minus or plus? If it's a plus then that is great, you have a bit of extra cash you could use for savings. If it is a minus, then this can change.

Take a look at your list of outgoings and see if there is anything you can cut back on or cancel. Subscriptions you don't use, downgrading a package, changing where you shop or what you buy.

Now an additional task for you is the cancel or change those subscriptions. This may take a few days but make a start.

Say your 3 THANK YOUS

Use this page to note down the subscriptions:

## DAY 18

**I have an abundance of money and am grateful for all money that I receive and pay out. Money comes easy to me and I love and cherish it.**

Now you know how much exactly your outgoings are, how much you receive each month and how much you want to save, let's go on a treasure hunt!

This is so much fun and you can get the kids involved too. Firstly, we are going to look for physical money around your home, in the car, workplace (in your area only and no stealing from the tills).

Look in pockets, under the sofa, in all the drawers, old purses and handbags. Collect all the loose change and notes if you are lucky enough to find some.

How much have you found?

Say your 3 THANK YOUS

# DAY 19

**I have an abundance of money and am grateful for all money that I receive and pay out. Money comes easy to me and I love and cherish it.**

Time to take action decluttering your space and getting rid of unwanted items!

My way of doing this is asking myself 'have I used/worn/needed this in the last year?' If the answer is no, then it is going!

Old books, DVDs, clothes, games, toys, gadgets etc anything you don't need and you could sell.

If there is something that you feel wouldn't sell then you can give anything to a charity shop.

Now you have your items (this may take a few days to get together and that's fine) list them! Downloads apps for DVDs and Books called Ziffit, Ebay, Vinted or plan to hold a car boot.

Say your 3 THANK YOUS

Use this space to list what you find and how much you will sell it for and mark it off as you do:

# DAY 20

**I have an abundance of money and am grateful for all money that I receive and pay out. Money comes easy to me and I love and cherish it.**

Nearing the end however there are a few more ideas I would like you to try. You can choose all of them or just 1 or 2, that is up to you.

Meal plan for the next week - plan every single meal you are going to cook and write your shopping list with just those items.

Have you cancelled those unused subscriptions yet? If not, then get to it.

Pay for your bad habits - have a bad habit you want to change or get rid of? get a jar and label it with that bad habit. Choose an amount you will put in there for every time you find yourself doing that bad habit. It soon adds up and you can get rid of that bad habit.

Research savings accounts. When looking for a savings account they can be quite mind boggling. Main thing is to think about if you want instant access or would leave any savings in there longer term (you earn more interest on these ones), look at a higher interest rate account and whether you want to save regularly in there or as and when. Some accounts you have to save a certain amount so best to check.

Shop around for your energy, broadband, mobile and home insurances. If you would like to see how much you can save through these services then I can help you with that, just give me a message and we can arrange a chat. If you have been following me, then you will know I am a partner with the cheapest energy provider in the UK and can also help you save on all your household bills (not TV packages or water though).

Say your 3 THANK YOUS

## DAY 21

You should know your affirmation by heart by now:

**I have an abundance of money and am grateful for all money that I receive and pay out. Money comes easy to me and I love and cherish it.**

Looking at the past week, on a scale of 1-10 (1 being crap, 10 being amazing) how do you feel about money now? Do you think your mindset has changed around money?

Do you feel that there is more work to be done? Be honest with yourself and mark your answer down

Has it changed since the start?

The End - but it doesn't have to be!

So that is it. Thank you for sticking it out for the whole 21 days. Hopefully you have taken some value from this and have started to take action and feel less scared and more in control when it comes to money.

When we are in control of things we are happier!

If you would like a chat about how I can help you save money on your bills then drop me a message. Also, if you are open to taking a look at earning an additional income in your spare time by helping others then again, give me a shout.

Always happy to help in anyway I can!

Happy saving!

www.themoneysavingmum.uk

## Bonus Content!

Below are some more money saving tips that will help you. plus, some ideas to help you save money and grab yourself my budget planner by visiting www.themoneysavingmum.uk and clicking Budget Planner.

Go To Bed When It Gets Dark
Going to bed for the night as soon as it gets dark is one of my more silly money saving tips. How do you save money this way? Well, by saving on your electric bills for starters.

Practice gratitude for expenses incurred - where appropriate.
The goal is to focus on "what the money has brought you, rather than seeing it as a deficit."
Doing so can help to address negative feelings related to money.

Just like we all see on social media about positive thinking, it is recommended when dealing with money stress too!

The 30-Day Frugal Living Challenge For 30 days, commit to adopting a frugal lifestyle by finding ways to save money in various aspects of your daily life. This could include activities like meal planning, couponing, energy conservation, DIY projects, and using free community resources.

Printed in Great Britain
by Amazon

27395408R00046